TABLE OF CONTENTS

JUMP PACK FALL 2017

DRAGON BALL SUPER

STORY BY AKIRA TORIYAMA, ART BY TOYOTAROU

Ever since Goku became Earth's greatest hero and gathered the seven Dragon Balls to defeat the evil Boo, his life on Earth has grown a little dull. But new threats loom overhead, and Goku and his friends will have to defend the planet once again in this continuation of Akira Toriyama's best-selling series *Dragon Ball*!

AVAILABLE IN PRINT AND DIGITAL
AT VIZ.COM!

FREE SIMULTANEOUS CHAPTERS

AT VIZ.COM/SHONENJUMP

...FORCED ALL LIFE ON PLANET EARTH TO THE BRINK OF EXTINCTION.

DARN IT!!!

THE SUDDEN APPEARANCE OF BOO, THE MIGHTIEST ENEMY OF ALL TIME...

BAM

HYAH!!!!!

HERCULE!

HERCULE!

HERCULE!

HERCULE!

HERCULE!

HERCULE!

HOWEVER, BY ANSWERING THE CALL FROM HERCULE, ENERGY ACROSS THE ENTIRE UNIVERSE WAS GATHERED AND FORMED INTO THE ULTIMATE GENKI-DAMA.

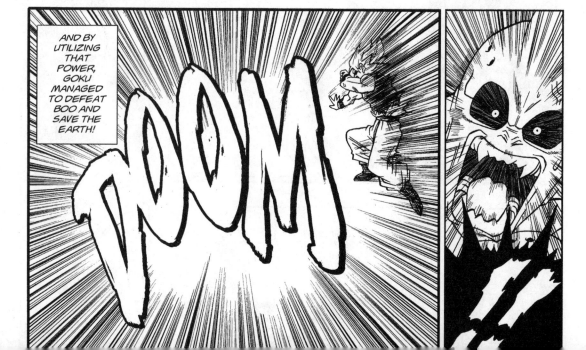

AND BY UTILIZING THAT POWER, GOKU MANAGED TO DEFEAT BOO AND SAVE THE EARTH!

DOOM

SKREE

KREEK

OOOOM

SSS

RATTL

WAH!

BWUH

KRASH

GOTEN! IF YOU DON'T DO YOUR JOB, I CAN'T FOCUS ON MY TRAINING.

SHOOM

GRAB

DAD, WERE YOU TRAINING BACK THERE?

WOW...

YOU ALWAYS GOTTA BE READY!

YEAH!

YOU NEVER KNOW WHEN ANOTHER STRONG ENEMY LIKE BOO WILL APPEAR AGAIN!

THUD

WOOSH

I HEARD THAT GRANDPA GYÚ-MAÓ IS TOTALLY BROKE NOW TOO!

HA HA HA!

I GUESS THE STRONGEST PERSON IN THE WORLD REALLY IS MOM!

FEH

HONESTLY, I WISH I COULD GO SOMEWHERE ELSE TO TRAIN, LIKE THE LORD OF WORLDS'S PLACE...

...BUT CHI-CHI KEEPS YELLING AT ME TO WORK AND MAKE MONEY...

YEAH, BUT WHAT I REALLY ENJOY IS TRAINING WHILE SLACKING OFF.

BUT MOM SAID THAT THERE ARE PLENTY OF MONEY-MAKING JOBS OUT THERE THAT YOU COULD GET.

JUST LIKE HERCULE DID!

MR. GOKU!

WHIRR

IT'S HERCULE!

OH! SPEAK OF THE DEVIL...

ON SOME PLANET IN THE UNIVERSE...

KINK KINK

BRING THOSE OVER.

HURRY, GENTLE-MEN!

YAWN ...

GULP

THESE, HUH ...?

THESE ARE THE FINEST DISHES OUR PLANET'S CHEFS HAVE TO OFFER.

PLEASE ENJOY, LORD BEERUS!

NOM NOM

...

MUNCH MUNCH

SNOSH

IT'S NOT BAD!

THE SEASONING IS VERY EXQUISITE. IT'S CERTAINLY TO MY TASTE.

GULP

DID YOU REALLY BELIEVE YOU COULD KILL ME WITH A POISON LIKE THAT?

BY THE WAY...

I-I SEE. WE ARE HAPPY TO HEAR THAT...!

HUH?

WAH?

IT HAS A MILD TEXTURE...

AH... THAT'S ENOUGH.

HOW ABOUT THIS SOUP D'SAIAN GAHD!

POISON!? H-HOW COULD I POSSIBLY?! I GUESS IT DIDN'T TASTE SO GREAT AFTER ALL...

SUPE... SAIAN... GOD...!

...!

UGH!

KLAK

DARN IT! WE HAVE NO CHOICE ...!

TOO BAD FOR YOU.

I THINK I WILL JUST DESTROY THIS PLANET.

VMM

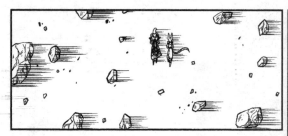

YEAH. THERE'S NO WAY I COULD LET THOSE JERKS KEEP BREATHING.

SO YOU ENDED UP DESTROYING IT JUST AS PLANNED AFTER ALL.

...YOUR DREAM?

IN...

...THE MAN I SAW IN MY DREAM...

BESIDES, I JUST REMEMBERED...

YOU'RE GIVING ME 100 MILLION ZENI?!

WHAT...?!

AND THAT AWARD CAME WITH SPECIAL PRIZE MONEY.

YOU KNOW, THEY STILL BELIEVE THAT I'M THE ONE WHO SAVED THE WORLD.

I WON THIS PRIZE CALLED "THE WORLD PEACE AWARD."

YOU WERE THERE TOO, AND YOU DID A GOOD JOB.

BUT I WASN'T THE ONLY ONE WHO FOUGHT BACK THERE...

PLEASE! DON'T BE SHY!

NO WAY! I DON'T NEED THAT.

THAT'S WHY I'M HERE.

BUT I BELIEVE THE MONEY TRULY BELONGS TO YOU FOLKS.

A THOU-SAND 100,000 ZENI?!

ONE THOU-SAND?!

LET'S SEE... THERE'S 1,000 OF THEM.

HOW MANY?

?

I CAN'T! I REALLY CAN'T TAKE SUCH A SCARY AMOUNT OF MONEY!

HOW MANY HUNDRED THOUSANDS ARE THERE IN THIS ZENI THING?

BUT, HEY...

YOU SHOULD LISTEN TO GOTEN.

MR. GOKU...

DAD, WHY DON'T YOU JUST TAKE IT? WITH THIS MONEY, YOU WON'T HAVE TO WORK ANYMORE AND MAYBE MOM WILL LET YOU GO TO KAIÔ-SAMA'S PLACE.

REALLY? BUT...

...

HMMMM...

THAT'S GREAT!!

WOW!!

I'LL TAKE IT THEN!

OKAY!

...I REALLY WANT YOU TO KEEP THIS BETWEEN US...

WELL... I'M NOT ASKING FOR THIS IN RETURN, BUT...

YOU SURE ABOUT THIS? THANKS!

OR SOME-THING LIKE THAT...

I COULD BE WRONG...

SUPER SAIYAN...

THE ULTIMATE WARRIOR WHO WOULD BE SO MUCH FUN TO PLAY AROUND WITH.

YES.

SO, YOU REMEMBERED THIS MR. SOMEBODY WHO APPEARED IN YOUR PREMONITION?

LET'S GO HOME AND TAKE MORE TIME TO CONSIDER.

MY, MY...

LET'S DO THAT.

...GOD...?

...THE SUPER SAIYAN GOD!

HE IS CALLED...

I HAVE A BAD FEELING ABOUT THIS...

HMMMM...

FORE-FATHER, I JUST SAW A PLANET DISAPPEAR...

...

IN THE LORD OF LORDS'S REALM

BORUTO: NARUTO NEXT GENERATIONS

CREATOR/SUPERVISOR: MASASHI KISHIMOTO, ART BY MIKIO IKEMOTO, SCRIPT BY UKYO KODACHI

Naruto was a young shinobi with an incorrigible knack for mischief. He achieved his dream to become the greatest ninja in the village, and his face sits atop the Hokage monument. But this is not his story... A new generation of ninja is ready to take the stage, led by Naruto's own son, Boruto! Times are now peaceful, and the new generation of shinobi has not experienced the same hardships as its parents. Perhaps that is why Boruto would rather play video games than train. However, one passion does burn deep in this ninja brat, and that is to defeat his neglectful father! In order to accomplish his goal, Boruto asks Sasuke to be his teacher...

2: The Training Begins!!

YEAH!

MAKE YOU MY STUDENT?

...DO THE RASEN-GAN?

CAN YOU...

HUH?

...

CAN YOU FORM ONE?

THE RASENGAN.

IF NOT, YOU CAN'T BE A STUDENT OF MINE.

I'LL GO MASTER IT RIGHT AWAY!

PIECE OF CAKE!

TAK

!

GUYS LIKE US...

NAH, HE'S DIFFERENT FROM HOW I WAS.

I GUESS, WE'RE BEHIND THE TIMES.

23

...

WE SHOULD OPERATE UNDER THAT PREMISE.

I SUSPECT THEY'RE MEMBERS OF THE SAME OHTSUTSUKI CLAN AS KAGUYA.

THOSE TWO...

...

YOU SHOULDA TOLD ME ABOUT THAT FIRST!

HEY, THAT'S A BIG DEAL!

CREAK

VWOOOO

THIS SURE LOOKS LIKE A HUGE LOAD OF TROUBLE...

WHAT'S THE BIG RUSH, EH, THIS EARLY?

ALL RIGHT ALREADY, EH...

MASTER KONO-HAMARU!!

MASTER KO-NO-HA-MA-RU!!!

PLEASE TEACH IT TO ME!!

YOUR RASENGAN, MASTER!!

I WANNA MASTER THAT JUTSU, LIKE, RIGHT NOW!!

HUNH ?!

34

YOUR HIDDEN ACE FOR THE CHUNIN EXAM!

YOU'RE PLANNING TO SURPRISE LORD SEVENTH, IS THAT IT?

HO HO.

YEAH! I GET TO BE THE ONE TO TEACH THE HOKAGE'S SON THIS JUTSU!!

I SWEAR TO FULFILL THIS VERY IMPORTANT DUTY, EH!!

OH, LORD FOURTH! LORD SEVENTH!

NOW YOU'RE FINALLY TALKING LIKE A SHINOBI!

I SEE, I SEE!

HEH HEH HEH

W-WELL, YEAH.

WHAAAA?!

COME ON, ONCE MORE!

WHAT HAPPENED TO YOUR ENTHUSIASM FROM EARLIER?!

JUST WATCH WHAT I DO CAREFULLY, THEN COPY IT, EH?!

SPEAK FOR YOUR-SELF!!!

QUIT SAYING "EH," EH!!

BUT IT'S NOT WORKING AT ALL, EH!

I KNOW, I KNOW!

MY LAST "EH" WAS REFERRING TO THIS BALLOON TECHNIQUE NOT WORKING!

I WASN'T COPYING YOUR "EH," OKAY!

YOU DON'T NEED TO COPY MY SPEECH PATTERN, EH!

...

ISN'T THERE A MORE EFFICIENT WAY TO MASTER IT?!

SPLASH

AND WHY START WITH A WATER BALLOON, ANYWAY?!

IT'S AN A-RANK JUTSU IN DIFFICULTY.

DID YOU THINK IT COULD BE LEARNED SO EASILY?

...SIX MONTHS OR SO TO PERFECT IT!

...AND ANOTHER...

GLUB

GLUB

...THREE YEARS TO DEVELOP THIS JUTSU...

IT TOOK LORD FOURTH, YOUR GRANDDAD...

VWW...

...

GOOD LUCK, GENIUS!

HERE!

PLOP

TREMBLE TREMBLE...

MURGH!

FLOP...

DARN IT! STILL NO GOOD!

PLMP

TMP!

!

...

CHIRP

CHIRP

WOW!

WHAT?! A RUBBER BALL THIS TIME?!!

KAW

NOW THEN...

FSH

...ON TO THE NEXT STEP, EH.

YES! I DID IT!!

WELL DONE!

NO WAY...

...EH ....!

N...

NHEEE

I DID IT!

HEH HEH.

!

*SIGN: UCHIHA

SWOO OOO

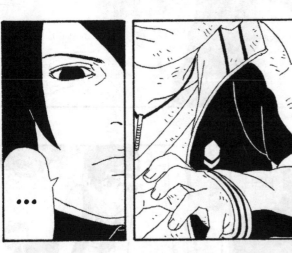

...

42

I'D BE HARD-PRESSED TO CALL THAT A RASENGAN.

!

IT'S AWFULLY SMALL...

I MASTERED IT, SEE!

WHAT'S SO FUNNY, HUH?!

HURL

DARN IT!!!

BUT...

!

UGH!

POOF...

SHWEE···N

UGH!

...

...

YOU'RE ALWAYS SO STRICT, DAD!

TMP

HUH?

YOU UNDERSTAND?

IT'S A MIRACLE HE EVEN MADE IT THIS FAR!

YOU'RE BOTH JUMPING TO CONCLUSIONS.

...LET ME TELL YOU, BORUTO USUALLY ISN'T LIKE THIS.

SINCE YOU PROBABLY DON'T KNOW HIM VERY WELL...

...

!

I WAS GOING TO MAKE HIM MY STUDENT...

I DIDN'T SAY NO.

PITTER PITTER...

HMPH.

*SIGN: THE CHUNIN EXAM IS HERE!

DARN IT.

BAH...

WHAT'S WRONG?

OH, YOUNG MASTER.

THAT'S TERRIBLE!

BUT IF THAT'S THE CASE, THEN I BELIEVE...

...OUR EXPERIMENTS HERE CAN BE OF USE TO YOU.

...GENE-RATION, SHOULD LOOK LIKE.

...WHAT THE NINJA OF THE NEXT, OF *YOUR*...

THAT OUGHT TO BE...

FSH...

SMARTLY...

COOLLY...

...AND EXPENDING LITTLE EFFORT TO PROCURE EXCEEDINGLY LARGE RESULTS.

FWOOSH

WOULDN'T YOU AGREE?

...LET US CHOOSE AN ULTIMATE MOVE THAT FITS YOU PERFECTLY.

NOW, YOUNG MASTER...

WHEN DID I GET SO FILTHY?

HUH?

WHAP

WHAP

!

WHAP

...

RASENGAN!!!

VWO OOSH

...

...WELL?

RASENGAN!!

HMPH.

...

I'M NOT LIKE MY DAD WHEN IT COMES...

...TO TALENT!

YOU ADVANCED THAT MUCH IN ONLY A DAY?

HEH!

THAT'S FOR SURE.

YOU SEEM QUITE DIFFERENT FROM NARUTO.

THOUGH I'D HOPED IT WASN'T THE CASE.

SHUP...

SHUP

IN TERMS OF MAKING ME YOUR STUDENT?!

SO?

WHAT'S YOUR ANSWER?!

HUH?

...

SHUP...

MY HERO ACADEMIA

BY KOHEI HORIKOSHI

Middle school student Izuku Midoriya wants to be a hero more than anything, but he hasn't got an ounce of power in him. With no chance of ever getting into the prestigious U.A. High School for budding heroes, his life is looking more and more like a dead end. Then an encounter with All Might, the greatest hero of them all, gives him a chance to change his destiny. Midoriya undergoes a grueling training session to prepare for the entrance exam to prestigious hero school U.A. High. But when push comes to shove, he has yet to score any points on the practical part of the exam. Could this be the end of his dream?

VOLUMES 1–9
AVAILABLE IN PRINT AND DIGITAL AT VIZ.COM!

READ THE LATEST CHAPTERS AT VIZ.COM/SHONENJUMP

IT'S JUST LIKE BEFORE.

THERE WAS ABSOLUTELY NO NEED FOR YOU TO PUT YOURSELF IN DANGER!!

THIS TIME...

OH...

WAIT. NO IT'S NOT!

I-I'M FALLING!! I'M FALLING!!

VOOM

BOW   BOW

OHHHHHHH?!

WHEREVER I LAND, I'M GONNA SPLATTER.

WAIT! WAS THAT ALL MIGHT'S POWER?!

IS THAT HOW I JUMPED SO HIGH?

NO.4 - STARTING LINE

FLAP

WHOOSH

OWWWWWWWWWW?!

?!

THROB
THROB
THROB

FLAP

SPLATTER?

ONLY BARELY... THIS BORROWED POWER!

I GOT CARRIED AWAY IN THAT MOMENT!!

I CAN ONLY BARELY CONTAIN IT!

IT'S ONLY BEEN TEN MONTHS!!

THIS IS ALL MIGHT'S POWER WE'RE TALKING ABOUT!!

THIS MUCH THOUGH...?! WELL, DUH...! I'M AN IDIOT!!

YOU MAY BE A PROPER VESSEL NOW, BUT... YOU WERE PUT TOGETHER IN A HURRY.

YOU'VE HAD NO TIME TO GET USED TO YOUR POWER... PREPARE FOR SOME REAL KICKBACK.

...ONLY BEEN GIVEN A PLACE AT THE STARTING LINE! THAT'S ALL!

I'VE ONLY...!

FWSH

FWSH

DETROIT SMASH!!

DETROIT

THINK!! WHAT DO I DO? WHAT DO I DO?!

URRRGHH!!

THROB THROB

WAAAAAGH!!

I CAN'T POSSIBLY PASS!!

TOO EARLY OR TOO LATE AND I'M DEAD! EVEN IF I PULL IT OFF, I'VE STILL GOT NO POINTS!! AND WITH MY LEFT ARM BROKEN...

BUT MY LEGS AND RIGHT ARM ARE SHOT!! GOTTA BE THE LEFT ARM!! IF I CAN AIM AT THE GROUND...! BUT TIMING IS EVERYTHING!!

FWUMP

?!

FWOOM

RE...

...LEASE.

TAP

FWOOSH

WHAM CRASH THUD

THROB THROB
THROB THROB

GAHHH-HHHH!

...

Bleargh...

Urp.

...!!

JUST... ONE POINT ...!!

URGH.

URGHH.

AT LEAST... THERE'S THAT!!

SCRAPE

CRAWL

IS SHE OKAY?! IS SHE HURT...?!

I'M SAVED...!! WELL...SHE SAVED ME!!

THANK GOODNESS...!

IT'S ALL...

...OVER!!

WHAT WAS THAT...?

WHF

THAT GUY.

...

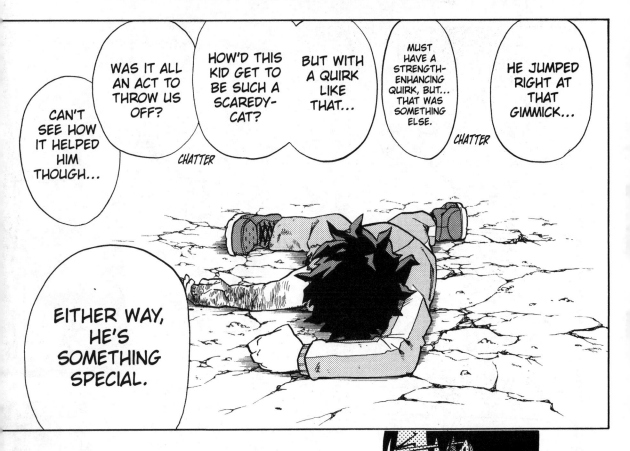

CAN'T SEE HOW IT HELPED HIM THOUGH...

WAS IT ALL AN ACT TO THROW US OFF?

CHATTER

HOW'D THIS KID GET TO BE SUCH A SCAREDY-CAT?

BUT WITH A QUIRK LIKE THAT...

MUST HAVE A STRENGTH-ENHANCING QUIRK, BUT... THAT WAS SOMETHING ELSE.

CHATTER

HE JUMPED RIGHT AT THAT GIMMICK...

EITHER WAY, HE'S SOMETHING SPECIAL.

THERE WAS A LOT TO CONSIDER...

A total mess!

He's all busted up!

WHAT HE NEEDED TO PASS.

THE REMAINING TIME... HIS OWN SAFETY ...

HE JUMPED IN TO SAVE THE GIRL!!

HE...

THAT'S NOT IT. WEREN'T THEY EVEN WATCHING?!

BUT HE DIDN'T HESITATE.

NOT AT ALL!

I WOULD HAVE DONE THE SAME!!

GLARE

I MEAN, SURE, IF THIS WEREN'T AN EXAM!!

YES, YES. HARIBO CANDY FOR ALL. EAT UP.

Thanks...

WELL DONE. GOOD WORK.

Huh.

OH?! THE EXAM... OF COURSE...!! COULD IT BE...?!

SHF

YES, WELL DONE.

SO YOUR OWN BELOVED QUIRK DID THIS TO YOU...

Oh my.

SHE'S THE BACKBONE OF U.A.

...?

FWIP

Oh.

THAT MADEMOISELLE...

GRANNY!

SMOOCH

?!

ALMOST LOOKS AS THOUGH...

...YOUR BODY ISN'T USED TO IT.

ANY OTHER HURT CHILDREN?

THIS ONE WILL BE FINE.

YOUTHFUL HEROINE
RECOVERY GIRL
[NURSING INSTRUCTOR]

IT'S IN LARGE PART THANKS TO HER PRESENCE...

...THAT U.A. DARES TO HOST SUCH WILD EXAMS.

HER QUIRK IS A *SUPER HEALING FACTOR.*

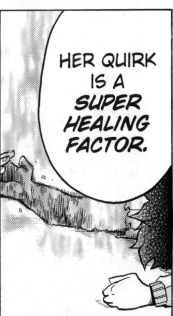

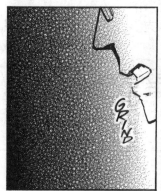

YES...! IF THE EXAM IS SET UP IN THAT WAY, THEN HE...

...

GRIND

ONE WEEK LATER.

IZUKU...

IZUKU?

ARE YOU OKAY?! STOP SMILING AT THE FISH!!

IZUKU?!

AH, SORRY... I'M FINE...!

BY MY OWN CALCULATIONS, I JUST BARELY PASSED THE WRITTEN PORTION.

FWIP

DAZED

BUT MY INCREDIBLE GOOSE EGG SCORE IN THE PRACTICAL MAKES IT ALL POINTLESS.

64

ALL MIGHT HASN'T CONTACTED ME.

KREEK

KREEK

...

AND SINCE THE DAY OF THE TEST...

I NEVER TOLD MOM ABOUT ALL MIGHT.

MHM ...

OH! YOUR DEAR OLD MOM THINKS IT'S WONDERFUL THAT YOU EVEN TRIED!

MHM ...

THE LETTER... IT SHOULD COME TODAY OR TOMORROW, RIGHT?!

...IT'D BE RIGHT, TO TELL MY FAMILY.

I DON'T EVEN THINK...

THAT'S A SECRET I HAVE TO KEEP. SO HE CAN GO ON BEING THE SYMBOL OF PEACE.

IZU- IZU- IZUKU! IZUKU !!

ALL MIGHT!! I DID WHAT I THOUGHT YOU WAN—

BUT... I DID WHAT I THOUGHT WAS RIGHT.

CLINK

ALL MIGHT! I DON'T KNOW WHAT YOU SAW IN ME. I'M SORRY.

IT'S REALLY HERE!!

THE LETTER!!

IT'S HERE!!

U.A. HIGH SCHOOL

FIDGET FIDGET

IZUKU

MMMM...

?!

...

URGH!!

RIP

THIS IS A PRO-JECTION!!

ALL MIGHT?!

IT'S BEEN A WHILE. THERE'S BEEN MUCH TO DELIBERATE ON.

APOLOGIES!!

AHEM.

HUH?! I THOUGHT THIS WAS FROM U.A.?!

HUH?!

FWIP

FWIP

WHATEVER I WANT TO SAY TO HIM...CAN BE SAID LATER?! AH, FINE. GOT IT...

WHAT'S THAT YOU SAY?! GET TO THE POINT?!

AT U.A.!! ALL MIGHT!!

I'M IN TOWN FOR ONE REASON ONLY.

I'VE COME TO TEACH AT U.A.

EVEN IF YOU PASS THE WRITTEN PORTION...

GETTING ZERO POINTS ON THE PRACTICAL...

... NATURALLY RESULTS IN FAILURE.

I KNEW IT! I KNEW IT! I KNEW IT, BUT...!

BUT THAT'S NOT THE END OF THE STORY!

I'M PATHETIC ...!!

PLEASE WATCH THE SCREEN!!

LET ME ENTERTAIN YOU!!

BEEP

Get on with it.

I HEARD HIM! THAT MEANS HE DIDN'T GET ANY POINTS, RIGHT...?

AT THE END, HE WAS SAYING, "JUST...ONE POINT!"

CAN YOU GIVE HIM SOME OF THE POINTS I EARNED?!

WHAT CAN YOU EVEN DO?!

AT LEAST HOWEVER MANY POINTS HE GAVE UP TRYING TO SAVE ME...!

THERE WAS ABSOLUTELY NO NEED FOR YOU TO PUT YOURSELF IN DANGER!!

AND YOU'VE MOVED OTHERS WITH YOUR ACTIONS.

YOU'VE ACQUIRED YOUR QUIRK.

HE SAVED MY LIFE!!

KL UNK

THAT BOY...

SLA SH

THIS EXAM, YOU SEE...!! WE WEREN'T JUST WATCHING FOR VILLAIN-BASED POINTS!!

THINK THIS IS ALL FOR THE CAMERAS?! THINK WHAT YOU WANT!!

IN THIS JOB, YOU RISK YOUR LIFE AND PUT YOUR MONEY WHERE YOUR MOUTH IS!!

A HERO COURSE THAT REJECTS THOSE WHO DO THE RIGHT THING...

...IS NO HERO COURSE AT ALL!!

BUT THERE SHOULDN'T BE A NEED FOR IT, MY LITTLE LISTENER!!

I'M AFRAID WE CAN'T GIVE HIM YOUR POINTS...

PAT

SIXTY POINTS FOR IZUKU MIDORIYA!

RESCUE POINTS WERE ALSO A FACTOR HERE!!

I NEVER THOUGHT... I...

YOU'RE IN.

AND WHILE WE'RE AT IT, 45 FOR OCHAKO URARAKA!!

ANOTHER FUNDAMENTAL WAY FOR U.A. TO EVALUATE YOU!!

THIS WILL BE YOUR HERO ACADEMY!

COME NOW, MIDORIYA!

SO BEGAN THE HIGH SCHOOL CAREER I'D DREAMED OF!!

YEAHH!!!

...!! RUB RUB

ALL THE HELP I GOT... IT'S CHANGED MY LIFE.

YU-GI-OH! ARC-V

ORIGINAL CONCEPT BY KAZUKI TAKAHASHI, PRODUCTION SUPPORT: STUDIO DICE, STORY BY SHIN YOSHIDA,
ART BY NAOHITO MIYOSHI, DUEL COMPOSITION BY MASAHIRO HIKOKUBO

On the mean streets of Maiami City, you've got to work hard to be the best. Yuzu Hiiragi and her father run a dueling school that's seen better days. If only they had a star teacher to bring in new students! When a rogue Duelist known as Phantom appears in the city, Yuzu may have found a savior, but Phantom will have to deal with the Leo Corporation's special forces before he can get into any community service! Things get complicated when people keep mistaking duelist Yuya Sakaki for the Phantom. The Leo Corporation orders Sawatari to bring him in anyway. Yuto's got some moves, but Sawatari's cards and monsters hammer Yuto almost into submission. Then a new Duelist appears!

AVAILABLE IN PRINT AND DIGITAL
AT VIZ.COM!

READ THE LATEST CHAPTERS
AT VIZ.COM/SHONENJUMP

AND NOW ...

...THE FUN BEGINS!!

YUYA SAKAKI
LP 200

THAT'S ...

WOW!

...THE PHANTOM'S TRUE IDENTITY!

SO THIS IS THE PHANTOM!!

A DUELTAINER, HUH?

HM...

FLUTTER FLUTTER FLUTTER

POM ♡

THE SLIPPERY LITTLE DEVIL!!

I ACTIVATE A TRAP!

REAWAKENING OF THE EMPEROR!!

REAWAKENING OF THE EMPEROR
(TRAP CARD)

Reactivate the effect of Advance Summoning one Emperor of Level 5 or higher.

THIS LETS ME REACTIVATE THE EFFECT OF ADVANCE SUMMONING AN EMPEROR OF LEVEL 5 OR OVER!!

WATCH OUT! HE HAS UNDERWORLD EMPEROR EREBUS, WHICH SENDS CARDS BACK TO YOUR DECK!

YUYA
LP 200

UNDERWORLD
EMPEROR EREBUS
ATK 2800

SAWATARI
LP 1500

NOW *THAT'S* SUMMON-ING!

HE SUMMONED A HIGH-LEVEL MONSTER IN ONE MOVE?!

GET **$5 OFF** YOUR SUBSCRIPTION!

WEEKLY SHONEN JUMP

1. Go to **viz.com/wsjoffer**
2. Sign up for an annual subscription
3. Enter the code below at checkout to get $5 off!

schltc201708

4. Start enjoying the official version of the world's greatest manga!